AF270942

Some
Awfully Tame, But Kinda
Funny Stories About Early
DAKOTA
LADIES-OF-THE-EVENING

by

Bruce Carlson

QUIXOTE PRESS
3544 Blakslee
Wever IA 52658
800-571-2665

i

© *1992 by A. Bruce Carlson*

Reprinted in 2006 and 2010

All rights reserved. No part of this book may be reproduced or transmitted in any form or by any means, electronic or mechanical, including photocopying, recording or by an informational storage or retrieval system, except by a reviewer who may quote brief passages in a review to be printed in a magazine or newspaper - without the permission in writing from the publisher.

* * * * * * * * *

Although the author has exhaustively researched all sources to ensure the accuracy and completeness of the information contained in this book, he assumes no responsibility for errors, inaccuracies, omissions, or any inconsistency herein. Any slights of people or organizations are unintentional. Readers should consult an attorney or accountant for specific applications to their individual publishing ventures.

QUIXOTE PRESS
3544 Blakslee
Wever IA 52658
800-571-2665

PRINTED IN U.S.A.

DEDICATION

This book is dedicated to all those grey-headed folks whose eyes turned backward so far as they told me of their stories, or those they had heard years ago.

Through these folks I learned of things I hadn't foreseen when I started this book. Memories of tenderness were shared with me. Recollections of the human spirit were brought here from the past.

Out of this, a fuller realization came to me that the kaleidoscope that is the human condition is one of many colors and patterns. We need to be careful lest we judge too quickly.

The reader must appreciate the fact that some of these stories could cause embarrassment to people living today. Because of that, some of the names used are fictitious. In those cases, it should be understood that any similarity between those names and actual people, living or dead, is purely coincidental.

TABLE OF CONTENTS

FOREWORD

These stories of DAKOTA LADIES OF THE
EVENING, rich in the range of human conditions
they present - deserve chronicling fully as much
as those of our more illustrious citizens (who,
after all, may have been among those ladies'
clientele). For in their stories is a mirror of the
more acceptable life the rest of us see. Along with
the fallen, the one-night stand and the cheap
booze are humor, creativity, sacrifice, and yes,
even love.

Professor Phil Hey
Briar Cliff College
Sioux City, Iowa

PREFACE

DAKOTA LADIES-OF-THE-EVENING is a book about those girls back around the turn of the century that practiced that age-old profession.

This isn't a book of passion, lust or heavy breathing. It's simply a collection of stories about incidents, situations, and people of a couple generations ago. These aren't profound stories of historical significance or cosmic importance. They're just stories that would have gotten lost if I hadn't gotten 'em down here. I hope you enjoy reading them as much as I enjoyed collecting and writing them.

CHAPTER I

HATTIE'S TURNABOUT

y the very nature of the business, the *"world's oldest profession"* has always claimed among its ranks a wide and curious assortment of humanity.

One of the more interesting girls ever to grace the garish interior of Miss Lena's House of Joy in Grand Forks was Hattie McGuire. Now, Hattie, bless her heart, wasn't exactly what you'd call a natural beauty. Fact is, she was so homely even a horsefly wouldn't look at her twice. And to make matters worse, Hattie had a wooden leg.

Hattie's artificial limb was the result of a train accident years earlier that killed both her parents and left Hattie hobbling down the road of life as best she could. Because of her physical deficiencies, the poor gal was painfully shy.

You might wonder how a young lady with such a timid nature ever found herself in an occupation that demanded an outgoing personality and usually encouraged a degree of ribaldry and rowdiness thrown in for good measure. Truth was, she fell into it quite by accident.

It was sometime around 1915 when Miss Lena found Hattie wandering the streets of Grand Forks. Hattie was lost, had no money, and no place to go. Lena took the hapless girl under her wing and told her she could stay at the House of Joy for the time being. Of course, the old madam was very careful to make sure Hattie understood exactly what sort of establishment she would be staying at. Hattie gratefully accepted Lena's hospitality.

A few weeks passed and the day came when Lena told Hattie straight out: *it was time to make a decision.*

Either she could mosey on down the road, or she could stay, learn the "tricks" of the trade, and be one of Miss Lena's girls. The feisty old madam wanted to be fair about it, but if someone was going to stay under her roof, they'd have to earn their keep. Can't blame her for that, I guess.

Lena laid it on the line. Working at the House of Joy, she told Hattie flat out, wouldn't be easy. The girl would have to pluck up her courage to overcome her handicaps. Sure, it would be hard, but with determination she could do it.

At first, Hattie wasn't too keen on the idea of working for Miss Lena. Not that she looked down on the other girls, or anything. Hattie just didn't have a speck of self-confidence about herself and figured she wasn't cut out for the job. Still, she knew she had to do something. In the end, she agreed to give it a try.

Hattie's initial attempts at socializing with the clients at the House of Joy were nothing short of disastrous. The fellas that frequented the place usually weren't the most debonair critters in the world, if you catch my drift. Not mean, mind you - just insensitive. Many of them were in the habit of imbibing a bit too much on the way and, consequently, were a mite short on tact. One of these charmers would invariably make a comment about Hattie's wooden leg, or her less than classic features, and she would bolt from the room in tears. One old geezer had the gall to ask Hattie what she was more afraid of there - bedbugs or termites? Her future as one of Miss Lena's girls seemed doubtful indeed.

That was before Jacob Fairdealer came to town. Jacob was a coffee salesman from Schenectady, making his rounds throughout the Midwest.

One evening he made an appearance at the House of Joy.

Jake sure wasn't much to look at: short, bald, with pale, watery eyes that peered through thick spectacles. On top of that, he had a peg leg.

You guessed it. Jake spotted Hattie and the two of them got along like two peas in a pod. As it turned out, they had a lot more in common than their wooden legs. Both were kinda shy and retiring and didn't have a whole lot to say. Jake did manage, however, to convince Hattie of one thing that night: success at anything can only come when you forget your limitations. Look at him - he had become a successful salesman in spite of his peg leg and his ungainly appearance.

When jake told Hattie that he thought she was

"purtier than a little red wagon," she was right in seventh heaven. Old Jake was very near-sighted, you understand.

Hattie's encounter with that coffee salesman from New York did wonders for her. From that day on, she came out of her shell and turned what she had once considered a liability into an asset. Hattie realized that being different sometimes had its advantages.

No one else in the business around Grand Forks had a wooden leg. That made her pretty darn unique. Once she realized how special she was, other folks took notice, too. Hattie soon became the most popular gal at the House of Joy.

Some say that Hattie stayed on at Miss Lena's for quite a while, that she even took over the House of Joy when Miss Lena retired.

Another version of her story says that Hattie ran off with Jake when he came back through town, and that she lived happily ever after back east as Mrs. Fairdealer. Which of these scenarios is closer to the truth, we'll never know for sure.

CHAPTER II

THE LOAN

 n the management side of the business, the award for the most enterprising and imaginative madam ever to operate a den of iniquity has to go to Ruby Mertz who operated "Ruby's" in Sioux Falls around the turn of the century. She recognized a golden opportunity when she saw one and wasted no time in taking advantage of it.

Ruby was pretty well known around town. One thing's for sure - you didn't mess with her. She had a reputation for being tough as nails. Ruby kept her house rules strict and her establishment orderly. She was first and foremost a businesswoman, and, like a true capitalist, her concern was profit.

That's why Mr. Hadshaw, the loan officer at the bank, took her very seriously when she sauntered into his office one day and asked to borrow two thousand dollars so she could upgrade her enterprise.

Ruby told the banker she wanted to renovate her existing premises, maybe build an addition. She also planned a trip to Chicago to recruit some new girls and basically improve her services to the community. Mr. Hadshaw listened carefully when Ruby insisted that she could pay the loan back in a year. She was so persuasive and seemed so darn confident that in the end, Hadshaw agreed to let her have the money.

"Ruby's" immediately underwent a dramatic face lift. It was a real eye-opener. Customers were surprised by the change in what had previously been a simple, modest sporting house. Now, brand spanking new black walnut and horsehair furniture was scattered throughout the establishment, along with imported Persian carpets, massive gilt-edged mirrors, and what seemed like acres of red velvet and brocade. There had obviously been a buying frenzy of tassels, fringe, and carnival glass.

In the meantime, Ruby made that little jaunt to Chicago like she said and returned with ten of the prettiest little gals folks around Sioux Falls had seen in a long time. Those honeys got all settled in, and business was booming for a while, at least.

Like any financial venture, though, things can go awry and your business can fall on hard times.

That's just what happened at "Ruby's". The first
problem to befall Madam Mertz was a new house
of ill repute that opened in the neighborhood.
The competition became fierce. The "Just
Reward" began an all-out advertising campaign,
promising reduced rates, free refreshments, and
even door prizes to gentlemen who chose to pat-
ronize their establishment.

The second blow to "Ruby's" came that summer
when a fraternal group moved their state convention to Rapid City. Ruby had been counting on
that convention revenue. Now, the year was

and the final installment of her bank loan would be due - along with the appropriate interest. How in blazes was she going to come up with the money?

Ruby pondered the problem for days before she finally had a brainstorm. It was so simple: she and the girls would hold some sort of carnival or fair. Folks in those days loved gaudy outdoor activities like that. The bigger and more extravagant, the better. They could set up this fair in the vacant lot behind "Ruby's"; each girl could run a booth, and they'd really rake in the money.

Everyone thought it was a splendid idea. All sorts of hidden talents surfaced as each girl proposed what she could contribute in the way of entertainment.

Vera was sure she could get her uncle, who was a magician, to perform at the fair with his trained dogs. Esther had once worked in a circus where she would dive from a fifty-foot platform into a horse tank. She was vigorously encouraged to revive such skills for the worthy fundraiser. Francine, it was discovered, could juggle and walk a tight-rope. There was certainly a place in the carnival for that. Girls of less athletic inclination could manage concession stands and sell ice-

cream, hot dogs, or beer. There would be dancing and drinking and enough hoopla and shenanigans to appeal to everyone.

At this point, Ruby came up with the best idea of all. She decided she would rent one of those big gas balloons with the basket attached under-

neath to give people rides. For the normal price of a room at "Ruby's". a fella could take one of the girls for a romp up in the clouds. It would be an airborne pleasure palace!

Leave it to Ruby Mertz to come up with an idea like that. Why, they'd make a bundle on the balloon ride alone.

The girls all got busy making preparations. They passed out hand bills and posted ads all over town. When the opening day of the fair arrived, the lot behind "Ruby's" was crawling with all sorts of curious folks. It was the first time in anyone's memory that a bunch of red-light gals put on a carnival.

Of course, the big attraction was the huge helium balloon Ruby had rented. Never one to do things half-way, Ruby took advantage of the advertising space and had a big sign plastered across it touting her establishment.

The festivities were proceeding smoothly, and folks were having a howlin' good time when things kinda hit a snag. A man in a high silk hat had just embarked in the balloon with the gal of his choice when out of the crowd emerged that man's disgruntled wife. Brandishing an expression on her face like a meat cleaver and waving a shotgun in her hand, the woman began bellowing obscenities and threatened to assassinate everyone involved in such wicked carrings-on.

Well, pandamonium broke out and people began running every which way. Some folks nearly got trampled underfoot. Luckily, that crazed woman didn't shoot anyone. What she did do was aim her shotgun at the big balloon and pull the trigger. Amid shrieks and screams from the crowd, that balloon exploded and the basket containing the girl and the wayward husband plunged to the ground like a rock. Neither were hurt since they had just taken off and were only about thirty feet in the air.

After paying for the balloon, Ruby and the girls were still a bit short of the money they needed for

the loan payment. They talked it over with Mr. Hadshaw at the bank, and he graciously gave them a little extension. It was the least he could do, so he said, when they had tried so hard. Besides, the man with the silk hat who was shot out of the air like some wild goose just happened to be Mr. Hadshaw's brother-in-law. It had all turned out for the best, Mr. Hadshaw said with a smile on his face.

So everything worked out, but as far as anyone knows, that was the first and last time any red-light gals ever put on a carnival.

CHAPTER III

POT LUCK

n the 1890's, no town in the Black Hills had a more notorious reputation or enjoyed its own dissipation quite as much as Deadwood. It was a real wild and woolly place and probably had more houses of ill fame than any town of equal size west of the Mississippi.

Because of the great number of these "service stations" and the many citizens who patronized them, not much effort was made to disguise the nature of the indelicate goings-on there. Everything was open and above board. Anyone who happened to stroll past one of these establishments and heard the boistrous activity amid the strains of the ragtime piano inside knew darn well there wasn't a prayer meeting going on in there.

The townsfolk were pretty tolerant in that respect. Even the local police tended to look the other way except in the most extreme situations. Of course, every once in a while, some do-gooder would come along and single-handedly attempt to reform the town overnight.

One such would-be reformer was Hiram Stokes. Hiram was an officer of the law, and he joined the Deadwood police force when one of its members retired. Hiram came from Kansas City, or some such place. He was plumb full of all kinds of new-fangled theories about big city crime and how to deal with it. With very little urging, he would talk your ear off about how he had saved towns everywhere from being swallowed up by corruption and vice. He vowed to do the same thing in Deadwood. I wouldn't go so far as to say that Hiram was conceited, but it wasn't unusual for his shootin' arm to be a mite sore - not from firing his gun, but from patting himself on the back for extended periods of time.

Old Hiram had quite an agenda. He was going to purge the town of crime wherever it might be found: in its saloons, its gambling dens, or its hurdy-gurdy houses. Right at the top of his list, though, was Deadwood's red light  district and the all-night gals who resided there.

One particularly lively night in the "badlands" (that section of lower Main Street where people went to have the most fun), Hiram and two other officers planned to make a raid on "Peg's", one of the more rambunctious houses down there in the badlands. At at a given signal, they burst through the front door, blowing their whistles and making all kinds of bothersome noises. Hiram was never one to do something in a simple, effective manner when he could make a big production of it.

As it happened, the officers had chosen that auspicious occasion to debut their new police uniforms, as well. Hiram had talked the department into the new regalia as a means of improving their image, something he had learned in the big city.

The costumes, which consisted of blue frock coats with lots of gaudy brass buttons and metal helmets only enhanced the spectacle. The girls at "Peg's" and their clients were more amused than anything.

The officers never did arrest anyone that night. It's pretty hard to intimidate someone when they're laughing at you. Something else side-tracked Hiram on his way to personal glory, too. Her name was Elly. She was the main attraction at "Peg's", and the moment Hiram laid eyes on her, his cold heart started to melt like a block of ice on the Fourth of July.

When Elly batted her big blue eyes and gave him a wink, Hiram forgot all about his self-appointed duty as dispenser of law and order. He forgot about everything except the cutest little gal he'd ever seen in his life. Hiram and the boys made a hasty retreat and  reported back to the police chief that they'd have to "study the situation some more."

Well, in the days that followed Hiram snuck back to study the situation every chance he got. Each

afternoon about two o'clock, he could be observed slipping in the back door of "Peg's", only to emerge an hour or so later looking like the cat who got the canary.

When questioned as to his whereabouts each afternoon between two and three, Hiram always insisted that he was out "walking his beat", protecting the citizens of Deadwood against criminal activity. Some of the folks around town joked that he was protecting the citizens by keeping the girls at "Peg's" - especially Elly -occupied each afternoon.

In any event, Hiram wasn't fooling anyone, no one except himself, that is.

The charade went on for about a month. People wouldn't have minded it so much if Hiram wasn't such a hypocrite about it. The thing was, he was always spouting about cleaning up the vice in town and then, without batting an eyelash, running to roll in the dirt.

A few of the men around Deadwood got together and devised a plan. At 2:15 one afternoon, a half dozen of them stood in the street directly in front of "Peg's" and proceeded to fire their guns in the air.

You can imagine what an awful commotion it made. The sound of all that gunfire echoed through the narrow streets of Deadwood and shattered the lazy afternoon quiet like glass. The guys figured Hiram would just have to come running out of that house to see what the devil was going on. Then, they'd have him red-handed. With all those witnesses around, he couldn't very well deny where he'd been or what he'd been up to.

Sure enough, Hiram heard the guns going off and thought that the bank was being robbed or a small war had errupted. It was his chance to see some real action. Of course, he knew better than to barge right out the front door. He figured he'd slip out the back, unseen, sprint down the alley to the end of the block, then circle around. He grabbed his helmet and was off.

By the time Hiram made it all the way around the block, Main Street was full of people. He did up the last brass button on his uniform just before he made his appearance.

"What's going on here?" he roared, surging through the crowd. Suddenly, there was five seconds of silence followed by a tidal wave of laughter. Everyone in the street seemed to be in hysterics. Even the girls in "Peg's" were leaning out the windows, hootin' and hollarin'. It took Hiram a little while to realize they were all laughing and pointing at him.

"Been out protecting us against crime, officer?" one old lady shouted in his face.

Then, it was all too obvious. In his haste to get outside, Hiram had reached for his helmet under the bed, only to grab instead the chamber pot. It was a big, white porcelain thunder mug with the word *"Peg's"* stamped across it in bold, black letters. You could have fried an egg on Hiram's face when he discovered what he had under his arm.

Needless to say, if Hiram Stokes had been slowly falling from grace in Deadwood for some time, he suddenly hit the ground with a dull thud.

Hiram didn't hang around for long. He was last seen heading west, making his way to another town where, no doubt, he spread it pretty thick about how he had cleaned up sin in the Black Hills. Things got back to normal in Deadwood after his departure, and the world's oldest profession flourished there for many years to come.

CHAPTER IV

THE FEUD

 peaking of competition, the rivalry between two pleasure studios in Aberdeen in the 1890's has got to be among the fiercest in the history of the profession. From the minute the "Jewel" opened up down the street from "Adeline's", things got pretty interesting.

"Adeline's" had been the only estab- lishment of that nature in town for a good many years. Adeline Baxter, the house-mother of the place, enjoyed her

monopoly in the community, and didn't take kindly to anyone else encroaching on her territory. Adeline's girls kinda took a dim view of the situation, too. They went out of their way to show the "Jewel" girls that they were about as welcome in the neighborhood as polecats at a picnic.

Some of the things the Adeline bunch did was pretty creative. One afternoon, they slipped a wasp's nest into the opposing team's outhouse and then blocked the door shut when one of the unsuspecting girls made the mistake of going inside.

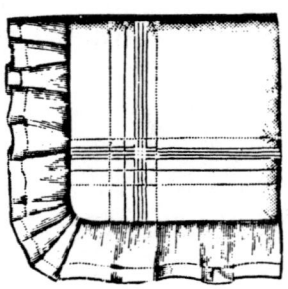

Another time, the crew from "Adeline's" sprinkled itching powder on all of the "Jewel's" bedding and linen as it hung on the clothesline. Later on, you could hear the cussin' and swearin' half way down the block.

Of course, there were the typical fistfights that broke out when girls from both establishments encountered each other on the streets. More than one lady sported a black eye for a while as a result of these skirmishes.

The whole thing came to a head on Labor Day weekend. That was always a busy time for the gals at "Adeline's". Imagine their surprise when the holiday came and went without a single gentle-man-caller making an appearance! Even their tried and true customers were scarce as hen's teeth. From the windows, Adeline and the girls could see prospective clients approach the house, then, at the last minute, turn and walk away. The girls even called to them, but to no avail.

It wasn't until the following morning that they discovered the reason for their rejection. On Adeline's front door, someone had painted the words in bright red paint:

MEASLES--
QUARANTINED

Then Adeline and her girls understood: it was that darn sign that had put them on the spot.

There wasn't much doubt as to who was behind it. It was the girls from the "Jewel" making the score a little more even.

Adeline and her girls realized then and there that all the dirty tricks they had played on their competition had just come back to them. It was obvious that one side could be as sneaky and conniving as the other. The feuding could go on indefinitely, so the only thing to do was bury the hatchet and try to get along. So that's what they did.

CHAPTER V

BIG BILL

owdays, everyone is familiar with the role competition plays in the business world. It's pretty simple: if you can't compete, you are out of business. It was a lesson Violet Beck learned back around 1905 when she became one of the girls at the "Pearly Gates" in Bismark, though she really didn't put it to the test until the following summer.

Now, the "Pearly Gates" was a real popular place, and, like most estabishments of that nature, the girls worked strictly on commission. It was real important, therefore, to put your best face forward when clients came calling.

It was, of course, more important to gain the attention and win the favor of certain clients over others. Sometimes there was a lot of bickering and hostility over that very concern.

Big Bill Taylor was one of those fellas the girls all looked forward to seeing. The minute word spread that Big Bill was in town, Violet and the rest of the gals would dash to their dressing tables to freshen up their spit curls and chalk their noses. When he made his grand entrance at the "Pearly Gates," they were on him like cockleburs on a dog.

Bill was one of those flamboyant characters, full of fun and frolic, who made having a rip-roaring time a top priority wherever he went. He smoked and drank too much, was an unabashed fanny-pincher; an all-around obnoxious guy. So why did all the girls flock to Big Bill?

He was rich - filthy rich and not the least bit shy about spending his money. The gal who landed that big galoot for the night could expect to be showered with money and presents as the evening and the liquor wore on.

Bill loved to dance. Weighing about an eighth of a ton, he wasn't exactly light on his feet, especially after being half-crocked on that tonsil varnish they called whiskey there at the "Pearly Gates." Still, when Bill was around, it was party time, and that always meant cutting a rug at some point.

During one particularly wild whoopee session, Big Bill announced that his choice of companion for the evening would be the winner of a dance marathon - a jigging contest to be exact. He had already narrowed it down to the two girls whom he considered the best dancers. It was Violet

against Nell, and both gals were game and ready
to go for it.

The match commenced in the parlor. Both girls
went at it with a fair amount of gusto for about fifteen minutes, and the onlookers could tell it was
gonna be a close one.

It had been sweltering all day, and the heat hadn't let up even after dark - which made the match even more interesting. When both girls were sweating so profusely that it appeared they had been dumped in the Missouri River, it was decided to move the festivities from the parlor to the front porch.

It was still pretty hot out on the porch, and the girls soon began shedding their clothing. In no time at all, neither one had on enough duds to dust a fiddle. Bill expressed his delight with loud hand clapping and sufficient cater-wauling and whistling to wake the dead, let alone the sleeping neighbors. Soon, everyone within a three-block area knew of the event.

The jigging contest ended after fifty-two minutes when Nell passed out and fell into the hedge that bordered the porch. She came to a few minutes later, a little groggy but none the worse for wear.

For her efforts, Violet won the attention of Big Bill that night. She did prove that sometimes you have to go to extremes to get the edge over your competition. Who knows? It might even have been worth it.

CHAPTER VI

NELLIE'S REVENGE

ife on the frontier was no bed of roses, that's for sure. Because conditions were so difficult, the citizens of any given town or mining camp did what they had to do to make their daily existence a little more bearable. All sorts of social activities and organizations sprang up among the people to fulfill this need. Churches, lodges, and clubs brought folds together and helped cement the community. Of course, there were always other interests as well, equally widespread, if not quite as respectable.

I shall endow the main character of this story with the fictitious name of Nellie Hawkins. Nellie was what could be politely termed a "lady of the evening," or, in the common parlance of that era, an "upstairs girl." Nellie's great-niece disclosed the details of her infamous aunt on the condition that no family name, past or present, be revealed. I shall respect that wish; hence, the alias, "Nellie Hawkins."

Nellie's domain was Miss Lizzie's Golden Apple, one of the many immoral factories in the Black Hills that sprouted around the turn of the century. Nellie was apparently a favorite among the clientele. Windblown prospectors and well-heeled bankers alike came from miles around just to see her. She treated everyone the same. Nellie's personality must have matched her good looks. Her hair was a rich, glowing auburn that was usually piled high on her head and she had green eyes that flashed emerald fire when she laughed.

Even the town's ladies bestowed upon Nellie a degree of tolerance unusual for gals of her ilk. There was often a cautious, though friendly, nodding when they passed her on the street.

When you're popular, however, it seems like there is always someone who is jealous. Some of the other girls who worked with Nellie envied her popularity and complained that she had the most spacious living quarters in the Golden Apple and enjoyed more privileges than anyone else. One day a squabble erupted between the auburn-haired beauty and another girl. Things quickly got out of hand and a push and shove match escalated into a full-fledged fist fight. The unfortunate incident ended with Nellie taking a nose dive down a flight of stairs. A broken neck ended her life and her illustrious career.

Those who dropped in at the Golden Apple were shocked and dismayed to hear of Nellie's fate. She was missed for a long while, but life goes on and things began to get back to normal. Or so everyone thought.

About a month or two after Nellie's passing, things started happening. They were insignificant things at first, hardly worth mentioning. No one would have even thought about making a connection between them. Eventually, though, it was obvious that a pattern was forming as first one girl, then another, got the bejabbers scared out of her.

Initially, it was just a matter of several misplaced articles. One girl's hat and gloves disappeared; another's diamond earrings were found in the bread box. The French perfume in a bottle belonging to one young lady was replaced by a curious substance that smelled suspiciously like skunk oil. As you can imagine, stunts like this really got everyone's dander up and the accusations aflying.

Other things happended, too. The lamp in the parlor would suddenly go on and off for no apparent reason, and mirrors, located in numerous places throughout the Golden Apple, would fog mysteriously.

The bizarre mischief would extend to the customers, as well. One gent who was leisurely enjoying his first warm bath in months nearly went into shock when a shower of icy water cascaded over his head and down his back. He cursed, sputtered, and looked around, but found no one else in the room.

By this time, Miss Lizzie and the girls were getting just a little bit perturbed by these goings-on. Not only was it downright scary, but it was bad for

business, too. The last straw came when a misty, vaporous form began to appear at the top of the stairs. It would stay there for a few minutes, then vanish. All who saw it agreed that the ghostly apparition looked very human-like and, in fact, bore a striking resemblance to Nellie Hawkins.

That was enough for everyone at the Golden Apple. The place was shut down and the girls all migrated elsewhere. It was never really proven that Nellie's ghost was behind all the misdeeds in that house, but that theory seems to make the most sense. The building remained vacant and burned to the ground a few years later, taking the secret with it. We'll just never know for sure.

CHAPTER VII

THE HONEY HUNT

ou don't hear much about it anymore, but back in the good old days, there was a practice that was pretty widespread if not widely known. It went by various names in different parts of the country. In some places it was called a "honey hunt," in others, simply "the roundup."

I recently met a fella from up around Huron who was kind enough to share with me his recollections of some "honey hunts" of years gone by. He did so on the condition that I not use his real name in the story; henceforth, he shall be known as " Sam." I asked Sam exactly what a "honey hunt" was.

"Just what it sounds like," Sam replied without batting an eye. *"They usually had 'em once or*

twice a year. A bunch of party gals - you know the kind I mean - would go and hide in the woods and the fields. Us fellas would go out on horseback and try to find 'em. We'd have our ropes with us, and we'd lasso the first gal we found."

"You'd actually take ropes out there and lasso them?" I asked incredulously. "That sounds kind of rough."

Sam laughed. "No, it wasn't like that. We wouldn't really tie 'em up. It was all fun, just part of the game. The gals had as good a time as we did. It was kinda like a big Easter egg hunt."

"Over how large an area did this hunt take place?"

"Oh, I dunno, probably a couple of square miles. Some of them honeys could hide real good, too. It might take you all day to find 'em. After they was all located, everybody wound up back at the ranch - that's where the girls lived - for a barbecue or something. It was just a whole lotta fun."

"Were there any ground rules?"

Sam thought a minute. "Well, as I recall, the gals had to wear bright clothes and always be in plain

sight when viewed from the proper angle. They couldn't move around. Let me see, oh yeah, the men couldn't use dogs to track 'em."

I almost had a feeling Sam was putting me on, but the whole thing sounded so crazy, I concluded that he had to be telling the truth.

"Did the festivities ever hit a snag?" I asked. *"Did anyone ever get into trouble?"*

Sam's eyes lit up and his face erupted into a broad grin. *"Yeah, as a matter of fact, that's why we had to quit having those hunts. We was right in the middle of one, having a good time, when one of the guys - I don't know where he was from; he wasn't a local guy - came across a cute little gal out in the middle of nowhere.*

He naturally thought she was one of the party girls, and he hauled her back with him. She was kicking and screaming her head off."

"She wasn't one of the party girls, I take it."

"She was the banker's wife who just happened to be out pickin' wild berries."

"She must have made quite a ruckus," I said, unable to suppress my laughter.

"She darn near scratched his eyes out. He should have figured that she wasn't playin' that game by all the fussin' and fightin' she was doin'. Lucky he didn't try to get too cozy with her on the way back to the ranch.

"Anyway," Sam said with fond regret, *"that was the end of our "honey hunts."*

I had to admit it was quite a story. First time I ever heard of wild berry picking in a head-on collision with wild-oats sowing.

CHAPTER VIII

PEACHES

 n the previous chapter, we saw how a verbal misunderstanding can sometimes lead to big trouble. Harley Grott found out the hard way that it usually pays to choose your words very carefully.

Harley's story goes way back to the early days in Northern Dakota Territory when the area around the Fort Union Trading Post and Williston was being settled. It was kind of a wild, disorderly place back then. One newcomer to the region observed that Williston, in 1887, had a saloon on each end of its one-block business district and about seven or eight more between them. That kinda gives you an idea of the role such institutions played in the socialization and dissipation of this early North Dakota community.

Along with the trappers, traders, and homesteaders who settled the area came the women of easy virtue. One of them, a cute little tootsie named Peaches, became well known to Harley, who was attempting at the time to establish a rudimentary newspaper in town. Harley had come west toting a printing press and a vague, optimistic dream about "bringing the news to the people."

Harley's early editions apparently weren't exactly paragons of journalistic excellence. Most considered them better gun wadding than reading material, and the issuance of these papers was erratic at best. Sometimes Harley's paper was a daily and sometimes it didn't come out for several days - depending on how much time in between he spent with Peaches.

Now, when the West was being settled, the men would frequently precede the women into any given area and try to civilize it to the point where the women, with their delicate dispositions and all, could comfortably move in. This was true of most women, but not all. After all, Peaches and some of her friends were among the first residents in town.

Thus, when Harley printed an item in his newspaper stating that the first "ladies" to move into the area would be arriving by stage coach on a particular day, the reaction of Peaches and the other girls was predictable. They seethed with anger. Of course, Harley hadn't meant to imply that, although there were females around, real "ladies" were in short supply, but it sure came out that way.

The day after the irksome paper came out, an unsuspecting Harley, with no warning of what was about to befall him, stolled into the establishment where Peaches and the girls worked. The moment he crossed the threshold, he knew he was in trouble. The gals were on him like ducks on a June bug. Peaches brought out a big whip and

proceeded to lasso Harley around the neck a few times. Then, the rest of the girls ganged up on him and, with a variety of lethal weapons from rolling pins to frying pans, punctuated the welts Peaches' whip had already administered.

Once they were convinced they had taught Harley a lesson, his assailants tore the clothes from his bruised, beaten body and chucked him out into the street. It was said that Harley lit out of town faster than a turpentined cat.

It just goes to show - never inpugn a gal's status as a lady, regardless of what she does for a living!

CHAPTER IX

FATHER SLOAN'S JUDGEMENT DAY

rs. Henry Cage of Peirre was pleased as punch when she received the letter from her brother in Boston informing her of his impending visit. She hadn't seen George for nigh on ten years, ever since he had been ordained a priest and sent to head a parish back East. Margaret Cage and her brother had always been close, so she looked forward to their reunion. There would be so much reminiscing; so many things to talk about.

Father George Sloan arrived in Pierre a week later and spent his first day there at the home of his sister. The siblings whiled away the afternoon hours, talking and sharing family gossip. A lot had happened in the time since they had seen one another. George told Margaret all about saving

souls in the big city, and she described to him her life as a midwestern socialite.

After dinner, Father Sloan announced that he would like to go out and see what sorts of cultural amenities Pierre could offer as compared with those of Boston. As he was leaving, Margaret jokingly told him not to stay out on the town too late because she had planned a luncheon in his honor the following afternoon. Several ladies from her club would be attending.

Father Sloan discovered that Pierre had greatly changed, and places 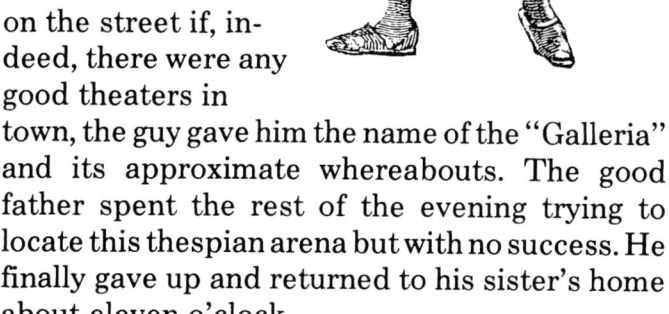 that he frequented ten years earlier seemed to have disappeared. He had always been particularly fond of the dramatic arts, so when he asked a man on the street if, indeed, there were any good theaters in town, the guy gave him the name of the "Galleria" and its approximate whereabouts. The good father spent the rest of the evening trying to locate this thespian arena but with no success. He finally gave up and returned to his sister's home about eleven o'clock.

The next day, at the luncheon given in his honor, Father Sloan was asked by one of Margaret's hobnobbing lady friends what he

had found to do in Pierre since his return. The priest unwittingly replied that he had spent the better part of last evening trying to find the "Galleria." For a second, that room became so quiet you could have heard a flea yawn.

Father Sloan hadn't taken into account the varied usage of the term "theater" in that neck of the woods. The "Galleria," of course, was not a legitimate theater at all, but one of Pierre's most notorious houses of ill repute.

Five ladies dropped their teacups right in their laps, two swallowed their scones whole, and poor Mrs. Cage fainted dead away. They all earnestly wondered what this world was coming to when a member of the clergy openly admitted that on his first night in town he had sought out a den of iniquity.

It was reported that Father Sloan's visit was cut a wee bit short. He returned to Boston a little sadder, but a little wiser, too, as to the nuances of the midwestern vernacular.

CHAPTER X

WHERE THERE'S SMOKE

 nother interesting story about ladies of the evening comes from the Black Hills where, it seems, ladies in that particular line of work were seldom in short supply. The incident happened in a small town, apparently somewhere between Hill City and Lead - that's as specific as my source of information could get. The town is gone now, but the story fortunately survived.

Each spring, it seems, the town's firemen would have their annual picnic and get-together. This little wing-ding was pretty tame. The most rousing activity would be a heated baseball game or an equally inspired horseshoe tournament. After that, everyone would have lunch and then go home.

This social gathering became somewhat of a tradition for the firemen and their families; year after year it was more or less the same thing. To put it bluntly, it got to be pretty darn boring. One year when they began making plans for their spring gala, someone made a suggestion.

He spoke for everyone when he said he thought the fellas were getting a mite tired of the same old horseshoe pitching contest and picnic lunch. Why not try something really different this time around? Why, he proposed, couldn't they take a little trip to Deadwood and visit one of them there bawdyhouses where all the "fallen women" stay. That sure would break the monotony, and it'd be a heckuva lot more fun than an old baseball game in the city park.

This brave soul's suggestion was met with a round of applause. The only thing was, how were they gonna get away with it? It would cost an arm and a leg to make such a trip. Besides, what would they tell their wives? There had already been a district convention that year, so they couldn't hardly use that as an excuse. And wouldn't everyone in town be just a tad bit curious when they discovered that the whole volunteer fire department had up and skipped town?

The men mulled over the situation for some time before one of 'em hit upon an idea. If you couldn't get to the fun, why not bring the fun to you? Maybe, just maybe, they could arrange to have them gals imported from Deadwood for a night of frolic. They could stay right there in the firehouse. The wives could be told it was an all-night drill or something, and no one would have to know any different.

Well, that sounded like a winner. The fire chief said he would send a letter right away to one of the finer sin parlors in Deadwood and see what could be done. If everything worked

out, the men could definitely look forward to a nice change of pace at their next get-together.

The chief made all the arrangements like he said, and the day fianlly rolled around when the shady ladies were to hit town. Elaborate plans were carried out to make their arrival as unobtrusive as possible. The stage coach was to drop them off about a mile from town where they could hoof it the rest of the way. The gals were suppposed to get to the fire station about midnight.

The firemen began gearing up for the rendezvous early on. In plain terms, they had been hitting the booze pretty heavy all evening, and by the time the female company showed up, several of the fellas were so drunk they couldn't have hit the ground with their hats in three tries.

The ladies were already kinda burned up about not having anyone to meet them when the stage dropped them off. They complained bitterly that they'd had to make their way to town in the dark and search out the fire station on their own. Now, on top of that, they find their companions for the evening soused to the gills. What kind of a bum deal had they gotten into?

The answer to that came about ten minutes later when shouts of *"Fire! Fire!"* suddenly cut through the calm night air. Then, there were more shouts and the smell of smoke. The honeys from Deadwood looked out the window. Sure enough, a building on the opposite end of Main Street was ablaze.

The ladies looked at the pickled firemen, most of whom by that time were out like a light, then, they looked at each other. It was pretty obvious there was only one thing to do.

Without wasting another word the ladies hitched up the team of horses to the fire engine, got everything all ready, and raced to the fire.

To say that the townspeople were thunderstruck to see their fire engine "manned" by what were obviously ladies of the evening all decked out in their party clothes would be putting it mildly. The important thing, though, was that the fire was promptly extinguished. Thanks to the quick actions of the girls, no one was hurt, and the livery stable, where the fire had started in a straw pile from an overturned lantern, sustained only moderate damage. Everyone commended the girls and expressed their gratitude; everyone except the inebriated firemen back at the station.

As you can probably guess, the next morning all hell broke loose. The all-night gals had high-tailed it back to Deadwood, and all that was left to remind the firemen of the missed night of fun were headaches so big they wouldn't fit in horse corrals. Not only that, but when they worked up  the courage to crawl back home, many of them got whopped black and blue by their wives. It was reported that the following year, the guys were back to pitching horseshoes.

No one ever let those firemen forget about their night of infamy, the night when a bunch of gals had to save the town. Kinda brings a new meaning to the phrase, "a hot time in the old town tonight," doesn't it?

CHAPTER XI

TWO JOBS

 olks back in '08 in Fargo sure weren't any different than anywhere else or any time else. They did what they had to in order to make a living.

Joyce Tenner's way was to run her combination house-of-ill-fame and sign painting service. Now,

that may seem like a bit of an odd combination, but, like I say, folks did what they had to.

Actually, Joyce started out simply as a sign painter. She had a flair for that and had done it for some time. Folks in Fargo were enjoying the same good times that others were throughout the Dakotas and lots of new businesses were starting up. Every one of those new businesses needed signs to declare their reason for being.

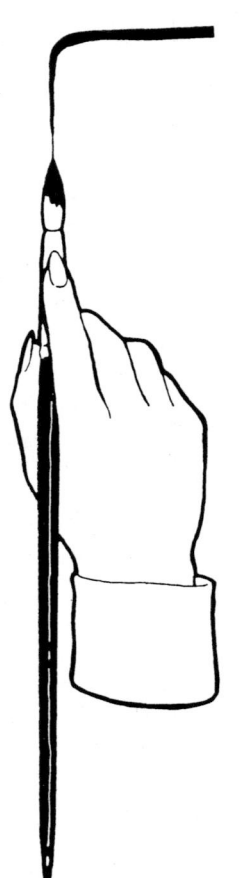

It was the Ladies-Of-The-Evening business that Joyce just kind of eased into: kind of a corporate in-house diversification, don't ya know.

So, from those two vocations grew an establishment there on the seedy side of Fargo that offered a couple different services to the citizens of fair Fargo.

This business kept things humming right along for Joyce and the three girls she had. True to her own instincts, Joyce taught those girls the elements of making good-looking signs, too. What with four good sign painters working at least half their time, coming up with their works of art, Joyce was able to do quite a bit of business.

There was some conflict among reports of the legality of the business there with the girls. Either the whole thing is illegal or the law enforcement

people simply tried to discourage it now and then.

Whatever the situation, Joyce was getting some heat from the local law there in Fargo about those girls.

At first blush it seems kind of strange that Joyce would have such a ratty and bedraggled sign advertising her own place. It was simply an old board with one end gnawed off by dry rot. The letters "GIRLS" and the accompanying arrow point to Joyce's house were crudely gouged out of that board. Some paint filled into those gouges sort of rounded the whole thing out.

It was, indeed, a ratty sign, and in stark contrast to the beautiful works of art that Joyce sold to the other local businesses. That ugly sign half a block from Joyce's worked but certainly didn't look very good.

But Joyce knew what she was doing, and that sign served her well.

When the law came calling about allegations of her running girls there at her place of business, Joyce would hotly protest her innocence.

"The people comin' and goin' around here are the fellows I'm makin' signs for, or are guys askin' about my doin' that. Jus' 'cause people are always

comin' and goin' doesn't mean I'm runnin' girls here, ya know."

The questions about the three girls who were staying there were easily fielded with equal conviction.

"Those girls! Those poor homeless creatures way out here on this heartless prairie, all by themselves! Those girls are stayin' with me. They are

my guests! They certainly aren't girls like you speak of, Sir!!"

At this point the lawman brought out the heavy

artillery. With the air of a man who has his prey cornered and all but caught, he'd say:

"But what about that sign down the street that's 'apointin' up this way and says "GIRLS."

"The sign?"

"Yes, the sign, the one that tells about girls down this way."

At this point Joyce would assume her best "sign-painting" look and throw a scornful glance there in the direction of that ratty old sign.

"Are you tryin' to tell me that crummy old sign is mine?"

"Well,......yes. It does......."

"Sir, I certainly don't know who put that sign there or what it means. I'm in the business of making beautiful signs for folks. Does that sign look like something that I'd do?"

Well, there wasn't anything the lawman could say about that. Obviously it wasn't the kind of sign that a sign maker would use for her own business.

Yes, that ratty old sign served Joyce very well.

CHAPTER XII

THE MASON-DIXON LINE

 hen Madame Hopewell set out to kind of spark her place up with some decoration and such, she should have stuck to something a bit more traditional. She could have done French Provincial, or Colonial. She could have chosen Old English, or any one of a lot of other things.

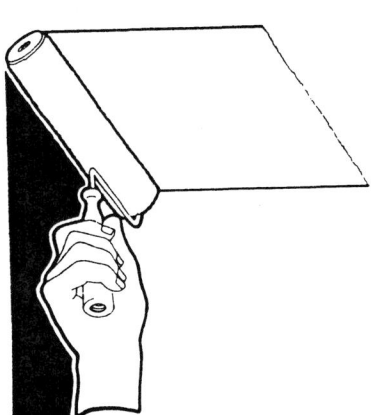

But, no, she had to go off and do something a little bit different.

Madame Hopewell proceeded to do a Civil War theme.

That Great Conflict had been over for thirty years already when she decided to do that Civil War decor there in her house of ill fame in Sioux Falls.

Lots of memories had faded through those thirty years and many passions had cooled about the Civil War. Madame Hopewell sure had no reason to think that great conflict with all its contentions wasn't well behind folks in 1895.

But she should have thought better of it. Memories of conflict die slowly.

In any event, Lucille Hopewell got her some confederate and union colors, posters, and such. One side of that large victorian parlor in her house of ill fame in Pierre Madame Hopewell gussied all up with the confederate stuff. She had all those flags and so forth dangling around. Right over the settee she had hung a portrait of Jefferson Davis, all decked out in his uniform and medals. It was enough to bring tears to the eyes of any red-blooded Son of the South.

And on the opposite side of the room, the

north side, the Union held supreme. A portrait of President Lincoln was flanked by other symbols,

all extolling the virtues of the Union. Among all this was, of course, the U.S. flag as it was in 1865, proudly showing its colors.

All in all, it was kind of an interesting room in spite of the fact that it was sort of militant, and hardly the kind of decor found in most houses of ill fame. Most such establishments, if decorated at all, were doing so in such a way to stir passions, but not exactly political ones.

Lucille Hopewell had done a good job of showing off the finery and glory of both sides of that tragic war. Time was to prove that she did too good a job.

Those passions that had laid beneath the ac-
cumulating years stirred anew within the hearts
of some of the older clients of The Hopewell
Haven. The sight of those old familiar faces on
the wall and those colors that had elicited such
emotion years earlier had their effects, even in
1895.

Even among the younger fellows, those re-
minders of the Civil War were far from lost. Most
of the young bucks had come to Pierre from back
east where the emotions still ran high in some
places. Most of the young fellows had lost a father
or an uncle in battle. The Civil War was far from
being over for an awfully lot of people.

It wasn't a question of whether or not the guys
there in that parlor would ever get into a real
fracus over that decor that Lucille had put up. It
was simply a matter of when it would happen and
how serious it would be.

And, within three months, it did happen. By
September of that year, the folly of Lucille's ways
was abundantly clear. That fight that broke out

between a couple of the old warhorses who really didn't have any business in such an establishment anyway wasn't a minor tiff. It didn't end up with just a bumped head or two. Those old duffers went at it driven with a fevor born of thirty years 'awaiting.

Now there were several young bucks in that place too, and they weren't about to miss out on a good old-fashioned knock-'em-down-and-drag-'em-out fight. It didn't take long for the finer points of the politics of the situation to get lost in the fun of a good fight. The flying fists were soon followed by

flying bullets from some dog-legs that seemed to appear out of nowhere.

What had started as a political situation, one inspired by the pictures of long-ago leaders looking down from the wall, continued as a fight made even more fun by the presence of a bevy of good-looking honeys looking on. Some fine-looking honeys watching can do more to enhance the quality of a good tussle than anything else, of course.

Fortunately, only two of the fellows even got nicked with that hot lead flying about. Jesse Winfield got a little corner taken out of his right ear. An unidentified client ended up with a couple of pieces of glass in his arm when a bullet shattered the bottle he was using for a settler-downer.

Lucille Hopewell learned a lot of things that evening. The most important of these was that even in 1895, a lady running a house for soiled doves had no business whatsoever goin' around inciting political passions that should have been dead for many years.

Another thing she learned was that a dozen properly inspired fellows could do a terrible lot of damage in an awfully short time. What she had there in her house that didn't get hit with a fist or

kicked got all shot up that night. Somehow all that flyin' lead that seemed to magically miss the human participants in the whole affair ended up sparing very little else in the building. Even the dog was said to have developed a permanent limp from the events of the evening.

While the farcas down at The Hopwell Haven wasn't

what you'd call the social event of the season there in Pierre, it sure turned out to be a lot of fun for the participants (except maybe that dog).

We don't know, now a century later, what Lucille Hopewell did after the Civil War, Phase II, but we can bet she picked out a theme a bit less controversial decor than a bunch of political stuff.

CHAPTER XIII

THE SANDS OF TIME

ost of the fellows who heard about it at first couldn't believe any such thing could be true. Most of 'em figured that for one of two reasons. One of those reasons was that gold dust wouldn't go through an hourglass. Why, everybody knew that it wasn't like sand that'd flow, kinda like, don't ya know. Gold dust had a way of kind of stickin' to itself. It would certainly plug up the little passageway from the top part of an hour glass to the lower part.

The other reason was that no matter what the talk was that came out of Deadwood, there simply wasn't any such critter as a lady of the evening that was worth spending time with while your gold dust was flowing through an hour glass. That stuff can add up pretty fast, you know.

Yes, most guys figured that talk about that house of ill fame that would let you stay as long as your gold dust would hold out in that hour glass was just that; just talk.

But they were wrong on all three counts. First of all, Madame Tillie had it rigged up so that gold dust would flow through the special hourglass she had there in her house of ill fame in Deadwood.

Yep, she had rigged up a treadmill with a big dog on it that would make a little arm keep a thumpin' and a thumpin' on the side of that hour glass. That little arm all the time thumpin' on that hour glass kept the gold flowing down the little passageway. The fact that the passageway was a bit bigger than in most hourglasses sure didn't hurt any, either.

Now, that little dog-powered treadmill was supposed to be for such things as running the handle on a washing machine, churning butter, or whatnot. It wasn't built to separate honest men from their gold dust. But that's what it did there in Madame Tillie's home for soiled doves back in one of those draws in the fair city of Deadwood.

That second reason that the fellows doubted that talk about Tillie's House about there bein' no such thing as a honey worth spending such a price for was dead wrong, too. Madame Tillie had a couple girls there that would not only knock a guy's socks off, but would just about make a fellow take to his cache of gold dust with a scoop shovel if need be. Those were a couple of right fine lookin' honeys.

And, last of all, it wasn't just all talk. It was a real live house of ill fame with a real live dog runnin' that hourglass thumper and more than a few guys poured all the dust they owned into the top of that hourglass without any second thoughts.

Yep, as long as a guy kept his dust running down into the lower part of that special hour glass they could stay with one of those two gals just as long as he wanted. Fortunately for the fellows' peace of mind, few of them were aware of how fast those tiny little golden flecks would slip through the hour glass. Not many of 'em spent a whole lot of time studying that hourglass, their bein' pre-occupied with other things, don't ya know.

A fellow wasn't allowed to put in just a little bit of dust. He had to fill the top part of the glass to the brim. If he wanted to leave before it all went on through, he could. All he had to do then was to dump the unused portion of the dust back out into the little leather bag the guys would carry their dust in, and then leave. But the rule was that he had to start out with that thing full.

No doubt but what lots of fellows went ahead and filled the hourglass, fully expecting to empty most of their dust back out. The girl's duty was, of course, to so captivate the fellow that he would soon forget those good intentions to rescue most of his dust.

And, of course, the poor guy who had been working or crousin' around too much and hadn't been gettin' enough sleep really ended up paying for his inattentiveness. Those guys would suddenly

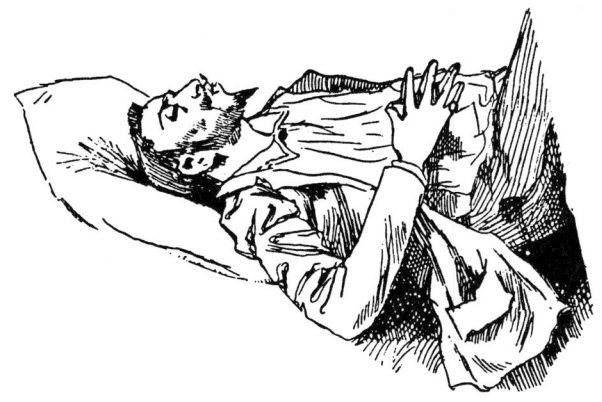

find themselves rudely awakened and being told in no uncertain terms that the dust had done run out. It's kind of tough, of course, to leap into a bed pretty well off one minute, and then wake up to bein' stoney broke a couple hours later.

One day one of the fellows figured he had a system to beat that gold-eating hourglass. He went to Madame Tillie's place of business armed with his coat pocket stuffed with little hunks of venison jerky. They were nice little pieces off the front quarter of a young buck and were right tasty.

This fellow would simply reach over every few minutes and secretly pitch a hunk of that venison jerky into the little cage where the dog was running his little treadmill. And the dogs do dearly love jerky.

The dog ended up spending about a quarter of his time walkin' that treadmill, and about three quarters of his time hunting around for any stray piece of jerky there in his cage.

Of course, as soon as the dog stopped walking, the treadmill would stop, and the little arm would quit thumpin' the side of that hourglass. It wouldn't take but a couple of seconds for that hourglass to plug up, giving our hero that much time free of cost.

The report was that the fellow was pleasantly surprised both at how well his little ploy worked and how the gal didn't seem to notice what he was doing. He was congratulating himself on how he was saving all kinds of gold dust with his investment of twenty-five cents worth of jerky.

But that fellow's preoccupation with keeping the dog diverted was, unknown to him, costing him very very dearly. The gal there with him was fully aware of what her guest was up to. She was kind of evening out the score by cleaning out the contents of his trouser pockets there by the side of the bed. She got several ten dollar gold pieces and a bunch of change.

So, it was the girl, Madame Tillie, and the power supply for the treadmill that came out ahead on that deal. That guy slowing down the flow of gold through the hourglass ended up paying dearly.

Between those two absolutely beautiful young honeys and the opportunity for guys to witness the cutting edge of technology, a lot of fellows poured a lot of gold dust into that hourglass.

Eventually that house of ill fame went the way of all houses of ill fame. Rumor had it that Madame Tillie left Deadwood with enough dust to buy a fine ranch out in California.

CHAPTER XIV

THE SURPRISE

'm just not real sure how early day city government worked back in the early 1900s here in North Dakota. Apparently, however, there was a variety of municipal government situations. For it was in 1908 that an election for Administrator was held in Point, North Dakota.

Perhaps the Administrator was much like a mayor, for the job wasn't one of several as if it were part of a committee or a council of some kind. It was the top job in town, and the office holder enjoyed the prestige of a powerful position.

That's a relative term, of course. You could be the top frog if you were Administrator in Point, but you'd just be the top frog in an awfully small pond. Point wasn't a very big place at all.

Small as it was, Point had its own house of ill fame. The Point Pleasure Palace wasn't the biggest or most prestigious such home for soiled doves, but it was doing alright. Many of its customers were fellows from nearby towns, and even towns off quite a ways. Point was a good place to kind of sneak away to. It was off in a little draw not too far from the Missouri River, kind of out of sight, don't you know.

There was kind of an unspoken and unwritten understanding between the city of Point and Point's Pleasure Palace. The girls down there at The Palace didn't go down to the city office up over the tavern to tell the fellows there if they should, or how to, run the city.

Likewise, the guys who would gather to jaw with the Administrator and his secretary every other Thursday night didn't bother the Pleasure Palace. That's not to say they didn't participate in the delights waiting there; they just didn't interfere any.

It was a comfortable relationship, one designed to enhance both tranquility and profit.

Several elections had come and gone in Point, none of which had elicited much noise or contention. Apparently, there weren't many burning issues in Point to get folks all het up.

Every now and then, of course, some situation would come up to add a bit of variety to things. In fact, every once in a while something big would happen to get folks a bit warm under the collar. For example, there was the time Eva Bradman shot one of Lester Wine's longhorns that wandered into her garden and violated the brussel sprouts. For a while there, Lester had about convinced folks that Eva'a garden threatened the whole cattle industry in North Dakota.

A couple of meetings were held over the whole mess, attended by Eva, Lester, and the entire staff of the city (the administrator and his secretary). It kind of took the starch out of the issue, however, when a romance blossomed between Eva and Lester. Before long those were Eva's and Lester's brussel sprouts. Those longhorns weren't Lester's anymore. They now belonged to both Eva and Lester. It's hard to whip up a whole lot of political passion about an issue when both sides are on the same side, so to speak.

But, that's all another story. I don't really want to get into that now. Back to the political climate in Point, North Dakota.

It was, for some reason, that '08 election when folks got to talking about The Pleasure Palace. There were a few revolutionary elements in town that questioned the social value of that place down there along the creek under that big old cottonwood tree. There was even talk that Point might be better off without that den of iniquity!

Of course, that kind of talk didn't set too well with the girls down there or with Madame Thomas

who was runnin' the place. There wasn't what you'd call just a whole lot goin' on in Point and the prospect of the end of The Pleasure Palace was no small matter.

Anger, apprehension, and cheap booze all conspired one night to move the folks down there to take some pretty drastic action. They decided they'd do a "write-in". They'd show those highfalutin' folks on the official nominating committee a thing or two! They'd run their own candidate. They'd heard all the talk about closing down The Pleasure Palace that they were going to! They'd show 'em!

Things got pretty exciting down there at the palace. Drawing up the papers replaced the traditional fist fights, and stirring speeches were made, laced with impassioned references to the constitution, motherhood, and everything that's right and true and strong.

Well, actually, the troops down there intended to go a bit light on the motherhood part. Learned discussions about Robert's Rules of Order replaced the gunplay that had theretofore been the second most favored activity at Point's Pleasure Palace.

It was democracy at its very finest. It made a lot of fellows proud to be Dakotans, Americans, and of voting age.

There was all kinds of strutting around and talking about The Will of The People, and how that wasn't gonna get ignored there in Point. It was all pretty heady stuff.

In all the to-do and excitement, the whole question of who to run almost got neglected. The issue got decided in a hurried and off-handed way by deciding to write in little mousey Annie McFarland. That was as much a slap in the face of the establishment as anything else. The troops there at the Palace wanted to make the point that anyone, just anyone at all, could win that election as long as she was backed by the most important institution in town.

A lot of bleary eyes and tobacco-stained fingers pored over the contents of Robert's Rules of Order to see if it might not be against the rules for a female to run for public office. Since no one could find anything that suggested it would be illegal, they went ahead and ran Annie McFarland.

Another factor that led the fellows to decide on Annie was that one of the guys recalled that the law required that a candidate be sober. And everyone knew that Annie had been found sober on several occasions. This fellow recalled seeing something about that in Robert's Rules of Order. The fact that Robert's Rules had nothing to do with candidate qualifications didn't seem to bother anyone. Maybe it was because most of the guys so busy studying that little book couldn't read a word.

With the dreary issue of who was to get written in behind the boys, the impassioned speeches and fine rhetoric could continue, and so it did. In fact, for a while there, Madame Thomas was a bit apprehensive lest political passions might eclipse the more traditional kind.

But those concerns of hers proved to be of little relevance. The booze ran out, and the cold light of reason the next morning sort of got things back to normal again.

Come election day everybody there at The Pleasure Palace reminded each other that they were all going to write Annie's name in for Administrator. They had, by that time, kind of turned the whole thing into a joke - but that was okay, too.

Now, wouldn't you know it, but when the big day came the whole political structure in Point was beside the point. Annie McFarland had a new job. She was now Point's official Administrator.

All that sort of set folks on their ears. The talk in the general store was about nothing else.

Three entire sermons were preached during the next month with the glum conclusion that Point was doomed.

The guys down at The Pleasure Palace all thought it was lots of fun, of course, and poor little mousey Annie McFarland was totally perplexed.

The change of office ceremony wasn't what you'd call real formal. The outgoing Administrator simply waved his hand in the general direction of the

wooden box containing the official papers. With an angry draw on his cigar, he then retired downstairs to the saloon to contemplate the inherent unfairness of life.

What does a mousey little lady of the evening do when confronted with the complexities of a city government and suddenly realizes that it was all her baby? Well, we don't know what most mousey little ladies of the evening do when faced with that situation, but we know the story of what little Annie McFarland did.

Her first move was remarkable enough. That gal actually took over: She quit her job down at the Pleasure Palace and moved into an apartment near the city offices up over the saloon. She fell to studying her new job and all it entailed. All that was, of course, pretty shocking to the folks in Point.

Those heavy legal books that had been used to prop up one end of the desk where the leg had gotten broken off were dusted off and carefully studied.

Somehow, Annie even got her hands on a typewriter and started to teach herself how to write letters on it, just like the folks in the city did it.

But even the novelty of such carryings-on as all that wore off as Annie quietly devoted all of her time to her new job. Little was seen or heard of her as she studied all those official looking papers and wrote lots and lots of letters to different people in the cities of North Dakota.

And, some awfully important looking letters came back addressed to Administrator Annie McFarland of Point, North Dakota. The guys in the saloon had all kinds of fits trying to figure out what was in all those letters. The fact that the saloon was the dropping off point for mail into Point offered endless entertainment to the regulars there.

A few of those letters that came to the saloon got a bit charred as the guys held them too close to the kerosene lights in an effort to read through the envelopes.

What was that woman up to?

But Annie wasn't saying. She just kept her nose to the grindstone, working all day, everyday on her new job. She even neglected her old friends down at the Palace as she immersed herself in work.

And, another funny thing was going on all this time. Annie got to lookin' less and less like she used to. She got herself kind of gussied up and fixed her hair differently. She looked and acted like a new woman. And, everybody agreed she was gettin' to be one fine-looking woman at that!

Even at that, though, things started to look like they were going to return to normal there in Point. Folks kind of got to thinkin' that she could engage in all the strange behaviour she wanted to, she wasn't gonna really make any difference in Point.

But that's where they were wrong. The seeds of change had been sown, the winds of a new age were already stirring the fallen cottonwood leaves in the streets of Point.

Things would never be the same again.

It was on a fall day that Annie struck. Folks woke up to find that the town they had grown so accustomed to no longer existed. There were whole new rules to play by, rules that came out of Annie's long hours at her desk.

That day taxes were levied under the

authority of the new administrator.

The secretary got a hefty raise. Permanent and rather nice new quarters for the City Office were obtained. New equipment and new supplies were purchased. Why, that woman even bought a second typewriter for the secretary to play.

If all that wasn't enough to get folks' juices 'a stirrin', Point's most important industry, The Pleasure Palace, found itself barred from further commercial activity within the confines of the city and had but thirty days to remove all of its property from the city.

No one ever knew how or why Annie did that, but she did. The Pleasure Palace was gone within a month.

Annie McFarland served three terms as Administrator with wisdom and grace before she resigned her office to marry a local rancher. Everybody agreed that that rancher made the best catch in the county.

Nobody, buy nobody, ever called Annie McFarland Sage mousey again, ever.

CHAPTER XV

OOOPS!

I n the fine old tradition of folks back in 1897, Loren Erickson fell in love, victorian style.

Loren may have been a few years late in falling victim to Cupid's arrows, but at the tender age of forty-five, he did. And, in the victorian tradition, he acted as if, and he maybe believed, the object of his affection was so pure that she was not even a woman in a biological sense. She was simply the embodiment of purity, goodness,

and whatever else a mortal could be. He had a pretty bad case of it.

And with that fiery red hair, the likes of which he had never seen, he figured that she was, without a doubt, the most beautiful creature that had ever existed.

When Loren fell into conversation with that lady in the general store, he was shocked to find that he had the courage to talk to her and to ask her where she lived. The lady's friendliness and gracefulness in answering just about made Loren so dizzy with excitement that he thought of nothing but that beautiful lady all week until he was scheduled to go to town the following week.

After getting to town there in Grand Forks, Loren prowled the area around the General Store where he'd seen her the previous week. He was hoping for the chance to see her again. He figured if she'd been at that store before, she might again.

Forture favored Loren. He had been there only an hour or so when he saw her. He was so much in love by this time that he would have haunted those wooden sidewalks all night to catch a glimpse of her, that beautiful Libby Hein.

Quickly, Loren maneuvered his way around to meet her again.

Normally Loren would have been so shy that he would have been paralyzed with fear in the presence of such a creature. But his desperate love for that gal and her amazingy friendliness and disarming manner made a new man of Loren Erickson.

He just about couldn't breathe with excitement when she invited him to her place for some iced tea. He agreed to do that, of course.

As the pair walked down the street to her place, Loren was so excited that he didn't see anything but that lovely companion walking beside him.

He was so distracted that he didn't see the red light out in front of her house. He had no idea he was entering a house of ill fame or that his new acquaintance was one of the girls working that place.

The two of them sat there in the parlor. Libby was a bit perplexed by her guest who was acting as if he was suffering from a severe case of stomach ache. Apparently she hadn't seen a man so in love that it was making him goofy.

Loren, meanwhile was just aching to once again see those beautiful voluptuous red tresses of his lovely hostess. In a fit of boldness that caught even Loren by surprise, he asked her if she would take her hat off. He just had to see that beautiful red hair again.

So she did, and her shawl, and her jacket, and her dress, and her slip, and everything else save one pretty smile.

Loren Erickson learned a lot that day.

CHAPTER XVI

THE WIG

f you look carefully at the underside or backside of some of those old antique overstuffed chairs, settees, and sofas you can often see a few strands of horse-hairs sticking out. Years ago they used the hair from the mane, tail and fetlocks of horses for furniture stuffing.

That hair is of larger diameter than most hair, so it's sort of springy. It doesn't do as good a job as modern materials for furniture padding, but proved quite satisfactory back in 1901 when comfort was one of the last considerations in furniture design. Like virtually every other house of ill

fame, the Fun Factory in Bismark used over-stuffed furniture poked full of horsehair padding.

Needless to say, gathering up enough horsehair to pad an easy chair was no small task. Lots of innocent hay burners were shorn to provide the hair for a nice large sofa.

So, when Madame Nolan there at the Fun Factory decided to repair even that small overstuffed chair, she was careful to provide herself with a large bag to slide the horsehair into so she could use it again after she had done the necessary repair work.

But that bag proved to be pointless. Through the years that great mass of horsehair all kind of meshed together into a hunk that held its shape even when the upholstery material was removed from the chair.

Carol Nolan was surprised to find that she could lift that large interwoven hunk of hair up off the chair all in one piece.

Carol was doing all this in one of the extra bedrooms upstairs where she could kind of confine the mess to one room.

As she lifted that mass of horsehair off that chair, she was struck by its appearance. The back and seat to the chair were almost a foot thick when it kind of fluffed up, released from the contraints of the uphostering material.

When she put that thing on the bed it looked all in the world like a huge wig. The "arms" of that chair pad looked like the hair that comes down on the sides of one's head. The seat and back of the pad made the top and back of the "wig." Yep, that chair shaped pad of horsehair looked like one giant wig. It looked like a wig that a gal would wear that could outfight a bear, outweigh an ox, and could do just about whatever she wanted to do without fear of anything or anybody.

Aside from the novelty of studying the similarity of that pad to a giant wig, Carol had lots of other things to do to spend a whole lot of time thinking about that.

She was glad, though, to see that hair kind of keep its shape so when she got the chair fixed she could just kind of reassemble the whole thing again.

Anyone who's redone an overstuffed chair knows it doesn't just happen overnight. Carol had been working on that chair for several days and still wasn't done. She was glad she had chosen to do that work in one of the empty rooms so she didn't have to clean up her mess each time she left it.

And one thing that wasn't any different back in 1901 than now is that before you can do anything, you have to do something else first. So it was with Carol, and that chair. She had left that disman-tled thing in that room while she did some stitch-ing on the upholstery.

So that "wig" laid in that extra room up there awaiting her return.

Meanwhile young Omar Wingate was walking back to the house from milking that morning. It was a bit of a hike from the barn with those two heavy pails and Omar was thinking about a con-versation he had had just the evening before with some of the older fellows.

Omar had acted like he wasn't really very interested as those older fellows were talking about the girls "for rent" at the Fun Factory in town. Omar had been amazed at what he'd learned the evening before. All three of those guys had been there at the Fun Factory, and what they talked about showed Omar there was a whole world out there that he was only dimly aware of.

Oh, he had known before last night about ladies of the evening. He even knew about the Fun Fac-

tory right there in Bismark. He sure hadn't known about all those fascinating details, though. That discussion among those guys gave him a whole new perspective on girls. He didn't know, for example, that some of what you see when you see a good lookin' girl walking down the street isn't necessarily all her.

Omar hadn't known about how girls could sort of round out their figures with extra stuff they could slip into their clothes. He hadn't known about wigs, false eyelashes, and so forth. He had just figured a girl was a girl. That previous evening's talk, though, revealed a girl could be a whole lot more than just a girl.

The milk in those pails just more than sloshed back and forth as Omar trudged along, thinking about another thing those fellows had mentioned. Omar was accustomed to girls being kind of shy and timid. All the girls in their little country school had been that way except for Lucy Norvick. She'd been kicked by a horse when she was just a kid and was kind of strange.

But those girls at the Fun Factory were all, according to those other fellows, pretty brash and not a bit shy. One of those guys even told of two of those girls who were always fightin' and how one of these two, a great big gal, had hit a guy so hard with a whiskey bottle one day that the fellow never was the same again. He ended up being' kind of punchy, just like Lucy Novick.

Girls fightin', jus' like men, now wasn't that something to think about!

By the time Omar got to the house and his mother's scurrying around getting the cream separator reassembled again after cleaning it kind of took Omar's mind off the Fun Factory, it was time to turn that crank and separate the cream from the milk.

A few minutes later, though, as Omar was turning the crank on that machine, his mind wandered again back to those girls at the Fun Factory.

The familiar and monotonous whirr of the separator kind of drifted Omar's mind off to thoughts of a world he had hardly even dared think about. It was a world of light and music there at the Fun Factory. It was a world of strange girls and things goin' on that never happened at that little country school he'd gone to. He thought about those rooms upstairs there in that house of ill fame where folks went, rooms that had seen things

Omar could only dimly speculate about.

Then Omar started to think about his little cache of money he had out in the oats bin from selling the hides from his trap lines.

Nobody knew that money was out there buried under the oats. So nobody would know if it were to disappear in case he were to take it to the Fun Factory and spend it.

By this time, Omar was done cranking, and he had made up his mind. That very next night he was going to go to Bismark to visit that place.

Omar had some difficulty going through the routine there on the farm during the next twenty-four hours. The more he thought about those lovely girls at the Fun Factory, the slower the time would drag.

Even time, determined to go as slowly as possible cannot prevent the coming of tomorrow, however. So that next morning Omar went to town *"just to look around"* he told his parents at the supper table.

Before long, Omar found himself nervously paying the woman over that little desk at the end of the hall and receiving his instructions as to where to go.

"Go to the top of the stairs, go left, and then go to the third room on the right."

By this time, Omar's mind was pretty much in a real turmoil. Here he was, right at the edge of seeing what a whole new world was going to be. Those words that lady spoke had to compete with a whole lot of other noise and all going on in his head. So Omar got those instructions exactly backwards. He went to the right and took the third room on the left.

Fate and improper listening led Omar right into the room where Carol Nolan had been working on

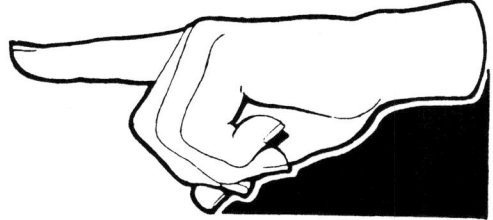

that overstuffed chair, and where that huge "wig' of horsehair was laying on the bed.

At first, all Omar saw was what appeared to be a normal bedroom. He looked onto the streets from the room. It looked so normal but Omar had the giddy feeling in his head that this wasn't going to be an ordinary day.

It was then that he turned and saw that thing on the bed. At first, it didn't even register. It was such a bizzare sight. He tried to deny what he was seeing was real, but he couldn't. There it laid, just as real a wig as it could be. There was one of those things that girls used to gussy themselves up.

Seeing his first wig was shock enough, but to see one of such huge proportions was all the more disturbing.

"Good Grief!" he thought to himself; *"That thing is monstrous."* Omar could hardly believe a human head could fit into that thing.

130

It was at that point that Omar recalled how the other fellows' conversation included things about those girls, and how short-tempered they could be. He remembered these fellows telling about how they would fight just like men.

Omar was accustomed to the idea of fellows fighting, he'd been in quite a few such things himself. But the idea of girls fighting was just about more than he could handle. He remembered those guys talking about that one really big gal that had caught a guy along the side of the head with a whiskey bottle hard enough that it had addled his brain.

All that came rushing into Omar's mind as he contemplated that huge wig on the bed. He knew that the owner of that thing would be coming into the room any moment! He also knew why he was there and that he was going to actually be tangling with that monster!

It was all more than Omar could handle. He wasn't about to tangle with whoever fit that wig. Whoever wore that thing was one tough customer, even if it was a woman. Suddenly Omar wanted to be gettin' out of there as fast as he could and wanted back to the comfort and predictability of the farm.

A quick leap out of the window onto the ledge below enabled Omar to drop to the porch roof and then to the ground. Within a matter of a minute, he felt the comfort of his familiar saddle and he turned his horse homeward.

So the life of Omar Wingate was not fated to cross paths in any kind of serious way with the fair sex that day. Without meaning to, a large hunk of chair stuffing laid on a bed convinced Omar the Fun Factory was no place for him.

CHAPTER XVII

OUT TO COOL

y the time the night was done, the fellow from over by the Missouri River who went to visit the lovelies way over at Aberdeen probably wished with all his might that he had never strayed from the straight and narrow that night. We don't know the guy's name, so I'll take the liberty of calling him John Doe. How's that for originality?

In any event, John sort of ducked into the back door of Madame Wooden's place that balmy September evening back in the fall of 1898. Apparently he had reason to conceal the fact that he was partaking of the pleasures of

Madame Wooden's house, yet he apparently figured he'd get away with it.

Things were progressing pretty well that night with John up on the second floor of that big old stone building. That is, things were progressing pretty well until John heard some commotion out in the hall.

Apparently that noise led him to believe that someone was looking for him and was determined to find him. Maybe it was a wife; maybe it was a girlfriend. We just don't know.

The reports of this incident tell however, what John did about the situation, and the difficult circumstances that John found himself in that night as a result of what he did.

John's instinct for self-preservation led him to frantically search for a way out of his predicament, or at least out of the room.

He apparently had reasons to feel he had but seconds to find a solution to the problem when he heard that noise in the hall.

John's eyes fell upon a huge decorative basket in the corner of the room. The thing was like a clothes hamper, but even larger. And instead of being made of reeds, it was constructed of small strips of wood. The thing had a lid on it just like the regular hampers. The basket turned out to be a storage chest for extra bedding, pillows, etc.

Quickly John dumped the contents of that basket out onto the floor and made a sort of sling out of sheets that he ran through the handles of the basket.

With a frantic glance at the door, John pitched the thing out of the window after tying one end to a heavy dresser. In an instant he followed that thing out, climbing down the sheet sling and hid himself in that gently swinging receptacle. Letting the lid flop down, John was able to fit entirely inside the thing.

Apparently John's fears were without foundation

because no one ever did come busting into that room looking for him. The honey he had been in there with closed the window to detract attention from it and then went on down the hall to see what the commotion was all about.

The commotion proved to be a drunk that had no

interest in John at all. The honey that had been up there with John had, by this time, found some clothes to slip on and ended up helping Madame Wooden and another gal pitch the drunk out into the alley behind the place.

What with all the excitement of getting rid of the drunk, and then having to forceably evict a stray dog that came in to escape the rapidly dropping temperature the thoughts of that gal were diverted from her client who was left hanging out of the window from that upstairs bedroom. As a matter of fact, she just plumb forgot about John out there in that basket with nothing on but his birthday suit in that increasingly cold night air.

Now, anyone who lives here in the Dakotas knows that really wierd things can happen in September. They know that a perfectly warm evening can suddenly turn into a downright nippy night. And they're probably even more aware of that possibility if they're hanging in a basket of an evening from a second story window and have nothing on.

We'll never know what became of John. All the folks had to go on was the evidence that remained the next morning when that gal suddenly remembered John's rather unique escape the previous night.

When that honey rushed back up to that room and flung the window open, she was greeted with pretty much the same sight that she saw when John had crawled into the basket the night before. She did discover, however, when she went to open the lid on the thing that it was securely latched shut. Apparently the little cast iron hook became engaged when John let that lid slam down. There was no way in the world that John could have gotten that lid open from inside the basket.

Gingerly, the little honey reached as far out of the window as she could to open the lid, really deathly afraid of what she would find. She knew that John had crawled into that thing. She recalled so well his doing that, wearing nothing but a worried look.

That little gal also knew how nippy it had gotten during the night. In fact, she was the one who insisted they build a little fire in the stove before going to bed for the night.

Would she find a client turned blue and frozen

stiff? What was under that lid. If he was dead, could they get her for contributing to that death? A million questions flooded through her mind as her chilly fingers worked the little latch to get that basket open.

It was one worried soiled dove that slowly lifted the lid to reveal what was inside.

Nothing. There was nothing in that thing. John was gone. But the way he got away was abundantly clear. He had apparently franically clawed at the thin strips of wood that formed that basket until he was able to rip several of them out enough to give him a hole to drop down out of to the ground below. It was a good eighteen feet below.

Unfortunately, for John, there was an embankment under him that forced him to drop a bit farther than he would have if the ground had been level under that window.

The folks there at the house of ill fame found nothing but some blood on the ground and John's wristwatch whose strap apparently broke from the fall. There were also some missing branches from some nearby bridal wreath hedge. It was speculated that John had concocted some  sort of garment from bridal wreath branches and had made good his escape.

Others favored the theory that John must have gotten seriously injured in the fall and crawled off somewhere and died. This theory sounded reasonable too, since no one ever saw the man again.

The "crawled off and died" school of thought also suggested that the coyotes must have gotten to him and hauled his bones off to a den somewhere where they had yet to see the light of day.

Maybe he died and maybe he didn't. Lots of folks around Aberdeen kind of kept an eye out for a ghost of a man wearing a suit made of branches of bridal wreath. As far as we know, one has never shown up.

CHAPTER XVIII

THE ERRAND

arney O'Neil had a little business going pretty well in the Black Hills back in '02 supplying firewood to quite a few businesses in the Rapid City area.

Most folks cut their own firewood for their homes, but the commercial establishments

would usually buy their firewood from suppliers like Barney. Most businessmen figured they could make more money tending to business than they could save by being out in the woods cutting their own firewood.

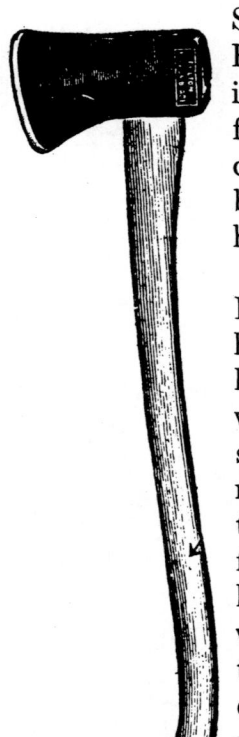

So old Barney did pretty well. He'd cut that wood and haul it into Rapid City just about as fast as his team of horses could keep it moving in that big old lumber wagon Barney had.

Barney always led a saddle horse behind the wagon when he'd work out in the woods. It was a lot easier and faster to simply throw a saddle on his mare and ride on into town than it was to drive the team in for every little errand he might have. Sometimes all he'd want would be a plug of chawin' tobacco or a drink. That saddle horse worked out real well.

Usually Barney worked alone, but on occasion he'd hire some guy to help him for anywhere from half a day up to a week at a time. Sometimes it felt good to work alone, and other times he liked having some company out there.

It was in the fall of '02 when Barney had Hans working for him. Barney found Hans in a saloon and didn't know much about his new helper, except that he was literally just off the boat from the old country.

Hans couldn't speak much English, and Barney not only didn't know how to talk Han's lingo but didn't even know what it was. Hans proved to be a good man with an axe, and that's all Barney cared about.

The two men got along pretty well, screaming what few words they had in common to each other. The rest of their communication was accomplished by gestures and signs. But that was no problem. It worked out well enough for them. Life in the woods cutting firewood wasn't exactly what you'd call high society, you know.

Things were going pretty well that fall day until late morning when Barney discovered he had left the little steel file back at the cabin. That file was just handy as all get out to sharpen the axes.

Now, anyone who'd done much wood cutting with an axe knows, it makes it a whole lot more work if the axe is dull. A good edge on an axe can just more than make the chips fly, don't you know?

Barney's answer to his problem was to send Hans to town with that mare to buy a new file. It was a lot closer to go into town to get a file than it was to go way back to the cabin to find the one he had meant to bring along.

So Barney proceeded to point to the mare and to Hans and scream the word "FILE" at his helper. No one really knows why folks who have a language problem seem to think that turning up the volume does any good, but folks do that, and so did Barney.

"File, File, Hans, File! Ride to town.....take mare; get file!"

Now, this wasn't the first time that Barney had sent Hans to town to get something. Several times already that week, Hans had ridden in to get some lunch, a bottle or two, some chewing tobacco, or whatever.

"File, Hans, FIle!" Barney repeated as he stuck some money under Hans' nose. *"File!"*

All the animation that Barney went through was designed to reinforce the words. He thought, from Hans' expression, that Hans understood what Barney wanted.

Barney may have hollered *"File!"* to Hans, but that wasn't what Hans heard. In his language that sounded just like what they spelled f-o-l-l-e in the old country, meaning; girl. Actually it meant "girl" as in the kind that hung out down there at the bordello by the creek.

Hans grinned and wagged his head up and down. He was more than happy to comply. Even having a break and going for a plug of tobacco was a welcome diversion from the rigors of cutting firewood. But to be sent to bring back one of those girls from the bordello was a chore he was more than happy to undertake.

Hans stood there eyeing the money that Barney had given him, not real sure what it would cost to get one of those girls out there and wondering if he had enough money to do it.

His studying that money must have made Barney think that he might as well have Hans pick up some lunch in town, too. So Barney stuck his fist back down into his pocket and came up with more money and screamed *"EATS"* to Hans.

"Ja" Hans said in recognition of one of the few words they had in common.

So off went Hans. He saddled that mare up and took off for Rapid City to get a girl from the bordello and some vittles from the general store.

Now, a girl from the bordello wasn't exactly what Barney had in mind, of course. He wanted a file for those axes. He knew that as soon as Hans got back he could put a right good edge on those axes again. Besides that, he was getting hungry. Just thinking about that food that he had told Hans to buy sort of got his stomach all set for dinner.

Meanwhile, Hans was feeling pretty good about this trip to town, of course. What more could a fellow ask for, but the chance to go to town for a nice-looking girls from the house of ill fame and some grub. It wasn't what you'd call bad duty for a fellow just off the boat from the old country.

The more Hans got to thinking about it, the better the whole idea sounded. Good old Barney! Barney had never sent him to town for a girl before. That's what you'd call a right good boss. Yes, sir, life in America was gonna be alright!

Hans thought briefly about his brother and cousins back in the old country. Why, they'd never have it so nice as things were proving to be here in America.

It wasn't long before, even at the slow walk that mare was accustomed to, Hans found himself riding down the street there in Rapid City.

The first thing he did was to stop at the General Store for some grub. While he was there, he even dipped into his own money for a bottle that the three of them could be nippin' at when he got that

gal back out there to where they were cuttin'
wood.

The next stop
was that ram-
shackle old
wreck of a
house where
those soiled
doves lived.

That money
that Barney
had given
Hans for the
file proved to
be insuffi-
cient for one
of those girls.
But, no mat-
ter. Hans was
feeling pretty
magnanimous
by this time
so he dug into
his pockets,
not only to
make up the
difference,
but to get a
second girl. It
was party
time now, and
who cared
about the

cost! After all, if the boss could be big enough to suggest some fun right in the middle of the day, Hans could go the extra mile, also.

So, that poor innocent mare patiently waiting outside the bordello found herself being called upon to carry quite a load on back to where the fellows had been cutting wood.

Fortunately, the girls that Hans had picked up were both small in stature. Even at that, and what with the pretty good-sized bottle and lunch, it made for quite a burden.

There was Hans in the saddle, a giggling girl behind him, and an equally pretty girl in front of him. The bottle was hanging with a cord from the saddle horn on the left, with the sack containing the lunch providing a counterweight on the right. In fact, there was just about everything on that mare except the file that Barney had sent Hans off for.

About fifteen minutes later Barney paused in his

work and stood there, axe in hand, listening for an odd sound he thought he had heard. Why, it sounded almost like a girl laughing and giggling, maybe even more than one of them.

At first Barney dismissed that idea and went back to loading up some of the firewood onto the wagon.

There it was again! It seemed like it was more than one girl. That funny sounding "clink-clink" sound was one Barney couldn't figure out at first, but the laughter was unmistakable.

Hans knew what that clink-clink sound was. It was the comforting sound of that bottle banging against the buckle on the cinch as the bottle swung back and forth to the cadence of the mare's walk.

Within a minute or two, the whole entourage came into the clearing the men had made in the dense woods. It consisted of one well-soused Hans, kept in the saddle by the efforts of two of the best-looking honeys Barney had ever seen in his whole life. There was one half-full bottle hanging like a cattle rustler from the saddle horn. And, last of all, there was a flattened and squashed sack that looked like it might have contained some lunch at one time. It was hanging on the other side, from the saddle horn.

One thing that Barney didn't see was the file he'd sent his helper after.

Now, it wouldn't be unrealistic to figure that Hans was about to enjoy the pleasures of unemployment right about then. There he was, drunk on the job, and didn't get what he'd been sent after.

Barney was a man of compassion, however, and he could understand that sometimes a feller can err. He found himself with all kinds of charitable thoughts, in fact, when that gal perched in front of that saddle smiled down at him.

Hans didn't get paid for working that afternoon. Far as that goes, neither did Barney. Not a piece of wood was cut and not a piece of wood got loaded onto the wagon.

It was one of Hans' funnest days in America so far. It was one of Barney's funnest days in America, too, and he'd been born and raised here.

EPILOGUE

So went life in America for Hans, or at least in the Rapid City corner of America.

And how about that homely hooker, Hattie McQuire, in Grand Forks? Who would have thought that a gal with a wooden leg could have done so well in the world's oldest profession?

And, odds are that Sioux Falls is the only town ever that saw one of its ladies-of-the-evening and her top-hatted client falling down out of the sky.

Those girls from back around the turn of the century are all gone now. But, if you listen real, real carefully, you can hear an occasional giggle from out of the past when life on the frontier was made a little more fun by ladies of easy virture.

If you have enjoyed this book, perhaps you would enjoy others from Quixote Press.

GHOSTS OF THE MISSISSIPPI RIVER
Mpls. to Dubuque by Bruce Carlson ....paperback $9.95

GHOSTS OF THE MISSISSIPPI RIVER
Dubuque to Keokuk by Bruce Carlson ....paperback $9.95

GHOSTS OF THE MISSISSIPPI RIVER
Keokuk to St. Louis by Bruce Carlson ....paperback $9.95

HOW TO TALK MIDWESTERN
by Robert Thomas........................paperback $7.95

GHOSTS OF DES MOINES COUNTY, IOWA
by Bruce Carlson ....hardback $12.00

GHOSTS OF SCOTT COUNTY, IOWA
by Bruce Carlson ....hardback $12.95

GHOSTS OF ROCK ISLAND COUNTY, ILLINOIS
by Bruce Carlson ....hardback $12.95

GHOSTS OF THE AMANA COLONIES
by Lori Erickson ....paperback $9.95

GHOSTS OF NORTHEAST IOWA
by Ruth Hein and Vicky Hinsenbrock ....paperback $9.95

GHOSTS OF POLK COUNTY, IOWA
by Tom Welch...........................paperback $9.95

GHOSTS OF THE IOWA GREAT LAKES
by Bruce Carlson ....paperback $9.95

MEMOIRS OF A DAKOTA HUNTER
by Gary Scholl ....paperback $9.95

LOST AND BURIED TREASURE ALONG THE MISSISSIPPI
by Gary Scholl and Netha Bell ....paperback $9.95

(Continued on Next Page)

MISSISSIPPI RIVER PO' FOLK
by Pat Wallace .... paperback $9.95

STRANGE FOLKS ALONG THE MISSISSIPPI
by Pat Wallace .... paperback $9.95

THE VANISHING OUTHOUSE OF IOWA
by Bruce Carlson .... paperback $9.95

THE VANISHING OUTHOUSE OF ILLINOIS
by Bruce Carlson .... paperback $9.95

THE VANISHING OUTHOUSE OF MINNESOTA
by Bruce Carlson .... paperback $9.95

THE VANISHING OUTHOUSE OF WISCONSIN
by Bruce Carlson .... paperback $9.95

MISSISSIPPI RIVER COOKIN' BOOK
by Bruce Carlson .... paperback $11.95

IOWA'S ROAD KILL COOKBOOK
by Bruce Carlson .... paperback $7.95

HITCH HIKING THE UPPER MIDWEST
by Bruce Carlson .... paperback $7.95

IOWA, THE LAND BETWEEN THE VOWELS
by Bruce Carlson .... paperback $9.95
(Farm Boy Stories From the Early 1900's)

GHOSTS OF SOUTHWEST MINNESOTA
by Ruth Hein .... paperback $9.95

ME 'N WESLEY
by Bruce Carlson .... paperback $9.95
*(Stories about the homemade toys that farm children made
and played with around the turn of the century.)*

SOUTH DAKOTA ROAD KILL COOKBOOK
by Bruce Carlson .... paperback $7.95

(Continued on Next Page)

GHOSTS OF THE BLACK HILLS
by Tom Welch..............................paperback $9.95

Some Pretty Tame, But Kinda Funny Stories About Early DAKOTA LADIES-OF-THE-EVENING
by Bruce Carlson..........................paperback $9.95

Some Pretty Tame, But Kinda Funny Stories About Early IOWA LADIES-OF-THE-EVENING
by Bruce Carlson..........................paperback $9.95

Some Pretty Tame, But Kinda Funny Stories About Early ILLINOIS LADIES-OF-THE-EVENING
by Bruce Carlson..........................paperback $9.95

Some Pretty Tame, But Kinda Funny Stories About Early MINNESOTA LADIES-OF-THE-EVENING
by Bruce Carlson..........................paperback $9.95

Some Pretty Tame, But Kinda Funny Stories About Early WISCONSIN LADIES-OF-THE-EVENING
by Bruce Carlson..........................paperback $9.95

Some Pretty Tame, But Kinda Funny Stories About Early MISSOURI LADIES-OF-THE-EVENING
by Bruce Carlson..........................paperback $9.95

THE DAKOTA'S VANISHING OUTHOUSE
by Bruce Carlson..........................paperback $9.95

ILLINOIS' ROAD KILL COOKBOOK
by Bruce Carlson..........................paperback $7.95

OLD IOWA HOUSES, YOUNG LOVES
by Bruce Carlson..........................paperback $9.95
*(Stories about old houses in Iowa
and young loves they have known.)*

TERROR IN THE BLACK HILLS
by Dick Kennedy .... paperback $9.95

IOWA'S EARLY HOME REMEDIES
by various .... paperback $9.95

GHOSTS OF DOOR COUNTY, WISCONSIN
by Geri Rider .... paperback $9.95

THE VANISHING OUTHOUSE OF MISSOURI
by Bruce Carlson .... paperback $9.95

JACK KING vs. DETECTIVE Mac KENZIE
by N. Bell .... paperback $9.95

RIVER SHARKS & SHENANIGANS
(tales of riverboat gambling of years ago)
by N. Bell .... paperback $9.95

TALES OF HACKETT'S CREEK
(1940s Mississippi River Kids)
by D. Titus .... paperback $9.95

LOST & BURIED TREASURE OF THE MISSISSIPPI RIVER
by N. Bell .... paperback $9.95

ROMANCE ON BOARD
by Helen Colby........................... paperback $9.95

UNSOLVED MYSTERIES OF THE MISSISSIPPI
by N. Bell .... paperback $9.95

TALL TALES OF THE MISSISSIPPI RIVER
by D. Titus .... paperback $9.95

TALL TALES OF THE MISSOURI RIVER
by D. Titus .... paperback $9.95

MAKIN' DO IN SOUTH DAKOTA
by various .... paperback $9.95

TRICKS WE PLAYED IN IOWA
by various .... paperback $9.95

CHILDREN OF THE RIVER
by various ....paperback $9.95

LET'S GO DOWN TO THE RIVER 'AN. . . .
by various ....paperback $9.95

EARLY WISCONSIN HOME REMEDIES
by various ....paperback $9.95

EARLY MISSOURI HOME REMEDIES
by various ....paperback $9.95

MY VERY FIRST. . . .
by various ....paperback $9.95

101 WAYS FOR IOWANS TO DO IN THEIR NEIGHBOR'S PESKY DOG WITHOUT GETTING CAUGHT
by B. Carlson ....paperback $7.95

SOUTH DAKOTA ROADKILL COOKBOOK
by B. Carlson ....paperback $9.95

A FIELD GUIDE TO IOWA'S CRITTERS
by B. Carlson ....paperback $7.95

A FIELD GUIDE TO MISSOURI'S CRITTERS
by B. Carlson ....paperback $7.95

MISSOURI'S ROADKILL COOKBOOK
by B. Carlson ....paperback $7.95

A FIELD GUIDE TO ILLINOIS' CRITTERS
by B. Carlson ....paperback $7.95

MINNESOTA'S ROADKILL COOKBOOK
by B. Carlson ....paperback $7.95

REVENGE OF THE ROADKILL
by B. Carlson .... paperback $7.95

THE MOTORIST'S FIELD GUIDE TO MIDWEST FARM EQUIPMENT
(misguided information as only a city
slicker can get it messed up)
by B. Carlson .... paperback $7.95

ILLINOIS EARLY HOME REMEDIES
by various .... paperback $9.95

GUNSHOOTIN', WHISKEY DRINKIN', GIRL CHASIN' TALES OUT OF THE OLD DAKOTA TERRITORY
by Netha Bell .... paperback $9.95

WYOMING'S ROADKILL COOKBOOK
by B. Carlson .... paperback $7.95

MONTANA'S ROADKILL COOKBOOK
by B. Carlson .... paperback $7.95

SHE CRIED WITH HER BOOTS ON
(tales of an early Nebraska housewife)
by M. Walsh .... paperback $9.95

SKUNK RIVER ANTHOLOGY
by Gene "Will" Olson .... paperback $9.95

101 WAYS TO USE A DEAD RIVER FLY
by B. Carlson .... paperback $7.95

FUNNIER THINGS TO DO COOKBOOK
by Louise Lum .... paperback $11.95

MAKIN' DO IN ILLINOIS
by various .... paperback $9.95

OLD MISSOURI HOUSES, NEW LOVES
by B. Carlson........................... paperback $9.95

YOU KNOW YOU'RE IN LOVE IN IOWA WHEN.....
by B. Carlson .... paperback $7.95

Index

Chapter Titles are in
Capital Letters

A

B

C

F

G

H

M

N

O

P

R

S

T

U

W

Y

NEED A GIFT?

For

- **Shower** • **Birthday** • **Mother's Day** •
- **Anniversary** • **Christmas** •

Turn Page For Order Form
(Order NOW While Supply Lasts!)

TO ORDER COPIES OF

DAKOTA LADIES-OF-THE-EVENING

Please send me _____ copies at $9.95 each plus $3.00 S/H each. (Make checks payable to **QUIXOTE PRESS**.)

Name _____

Street _____

City _____ State _____ Zip _____

SEND ORDERS TO:
QUIXOTE PRESS
3544 Blakslee
Wever IA 52658
800-571-2665

TO ORDER COPIES OF

DAKOTA LADIES-OF-THE-EVENING

Please send me _____ copies at $9.95 each plus $3.00 S/H each. (Make checks payable to **QUIXOTE PRESS**.)

Name _____

Street _____

City _____ State _____ Zip _____

SEND ORDERS TO:
QUIXOTE PRESS
3544 Blakslee
Wever IA 52658
800-571-2665